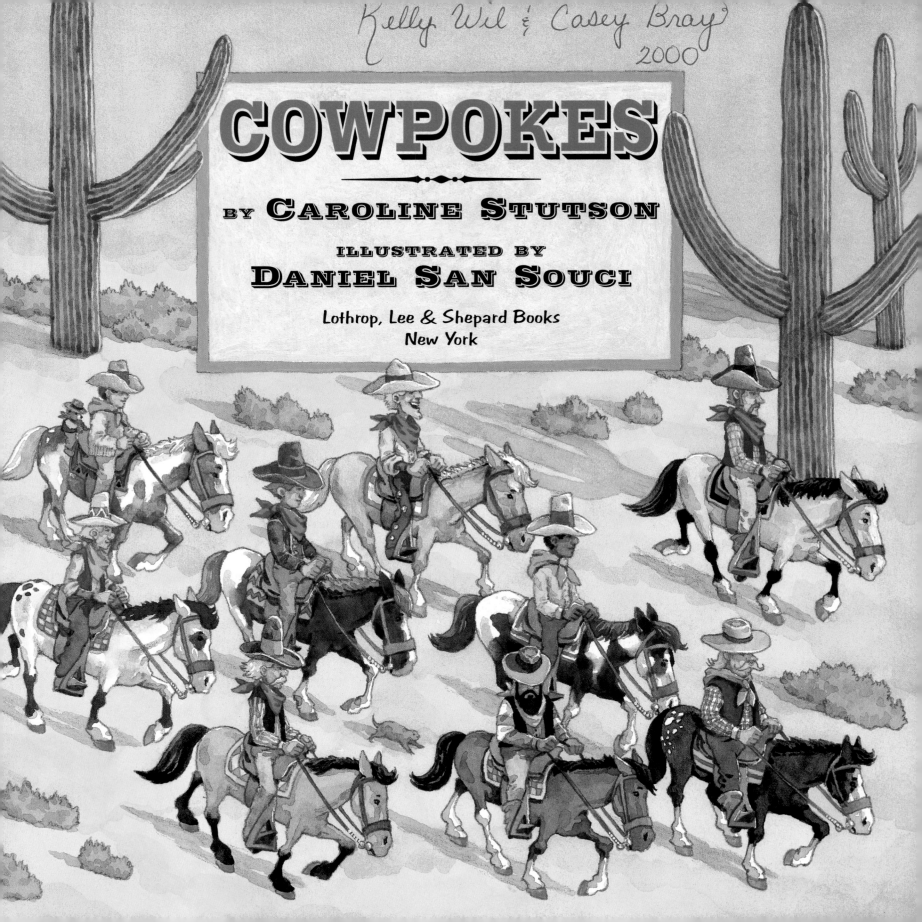

COWPOKES

BY CAROLINE STUTSON

ILLUSTRATED BY
DANIEL SAN SOUCI

Lothrop, Lee & Shepard Books
New York

Painted mountains at daybreak.

Rising slowly, cowpokes wake.

Austin's quieter than a hole
in the ground.

Slim's as slow as a snail
climbin' a greased log.

Elroy isn't overweight,
just a foot too short.

Bart, the boss, knows more about cattle
than a rabbit does about runnin'.

Tex calls on the ladies as regular
as a goose goes barefoot.

Boots and vests and leather chaps.

Curly took to cooking like
a bear to honey.

Justin tells jokes faster'n chain lightnin'
with a link snapped.

Marty isn't ankle-high to a June bug,
but he's cute as a little red wagon.

Cody's lived in the desert so long, he knows
all the lizards by their front names.

Billy can't tell skunks from house cats
without talking to Tex.

Bright bandannas. Cowpoke hats.

Eating flapjacks stack by stack.

Stirrup. Saddle. Up they go.

Practicing for the rodeo.

Through the chaparral and sage

on their ponies, roping strays.

Cowpokes branding, giving shots.

Then off the little dogies trot.

Mending fences when they break.

Cactus cushions!

Rattlesnake!

Back for supper—cowpoke stew,
beans and biscuits, cobbler too.

Guitars strumming. Shadows creep,

chasing star dogs in their sleep.

With love for Alec, the newest cowpoke in our family
—C.M.S.

For Joel Harris, a true friend
—D.S.S.

Watercolors were used for the full-color illustrations.
The text type is 28-point Opti Action Brush.

Text copyright © 1999 by Caroline Stutson
Illustrations copyright © 1999 by Daniel San Souci

Published by Lothrop, Lee & Shepard Books
a division of William Morrow and Company, Inc.
1350 Avenue of the Americas, New York, NY 10019
www.williammorrow.com

Printed in Hong Kong by South China Printing Company (1988) Ltd.

10 9 8 7 6 5 4 3 2 1

Library of Congress Cataloging-in-Publication Data
Stutson, Caroline.
Cowpokes/by Caroline Stutson; illustrated by Daniel San Souci.
p. cm.
Summary: Cowpokes wake, eat flapjacks, rope strays, mend fences, and
strum guitars, before falling asleep under the stars.
ISBN 0-688-13973-6 (trade)—ISBN 0-688-13974-4 (library)
[1. Cowboys—Fiction. 2. Stories in rhyme.] I. San Souci, Daniel, ill. II. Title.
PZ8.3.S925Co 1999 [E]—dc21 98-48137 CIP AC